Mathswork

By Steve Mills and Hilary Koll
Illustrated by Tina Barber

WAYLAND

Books in the series:

Mathswork 1
Mathswork 2

This book encourages children to read and helps them improve their literacy and numeracy.

✓ The contents page, page numbers, headings and index help locate specific pieces of information.

✓ The glossary reinforces alphabetic knowledge and extends vocabulary.

✓ The further information section suggests other books dealing with the same subject.

✓ Find out more about how this book is specifically relevant to the National Numeracy Strategy on page 31.

First published in 1999 by Wayland Publishers Limited, 61 Western Road, Hove, East Sussex, BN3 1JD, England

British Library Cataloguing in Publication Data
Mills, Steve
Mathswork 2. – (Mathswork)
I. Mathematics – Juvenile Literature
I. Title   II. Koll, Hilary
510

ISBN 0 7502 2545 9

find Wayland on the Internet at http://www.wayland.co.uk

Typeset by Mayer Media
Printed and bound by G.Canale & C.S.p.A., Turin
Colour Separation by P&W Graphics, Singapore

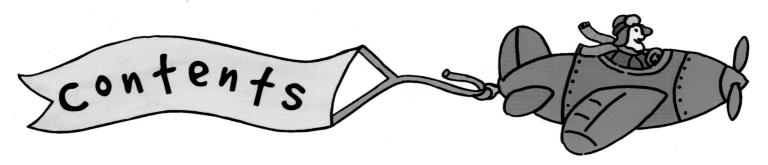

contents

Exploring Numbers

Josh has been keeping a diary. He has used numbers in all sorts of ways.

Secret diary – Keep out!

Saturday 26 January: Today I went with my Uncle to see Manchester United play Chelsea for my birthday present. I will be 8 years old tomorrow. Man. United won 3: 2. It was great! The ticket cost £20. There were 55,024 people at the ground. My mum let me stay up late and watch a film. I didn't go to bed until 9!

- How many different numbers are there in his diary?

- Put these numbers in order of size, largest first.

Look through a magazine or newspaper. How many different numbers can you see? Cut some of these out and make a poster of numbers of your own. Try sticking them in order.

Josh and his friends have been collecting numbers from magazines and newspapers and making a poster of numbers.

• Which are the biggest numbers and which are the smallest numbers?

Each of the numbers fits into one of the headlines:

• Can you work out which number might go with which headline?

One in a million

Amazing Facts

Here are some facts with very high numbers.

The biggest cheque ever written was worth **£1,425,000,000.**

The number of times your heart beats in a year is **37,000,000** times.

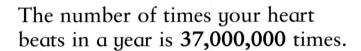

The number of times UFOs have been seen in the last 30 years is **100,000** times.

The number of kilometres the Sun is from Earth is **150,000,000** km.

The number of years since dinosaurs became extinct is **65,000,000** years.

• How many of the figures of amazing facts can you say?

Look at the table below to help you.

The number 37,000,000 is shown in the box below. It has 3 'tens of millions' and 7 'millions'. We say this number as 'thirty-seven million'.

thousands of millions	hundreds of millions	tens of millions	millions	hundreds of thousands	tens of thousands	thousands	hundreds	tens	units
		3	7,	0	0	0,	0	0	0

• Which amazing fact has the largest number?

• Can you put all the numbers of the amazing facts in order from the biggest to the smallest?

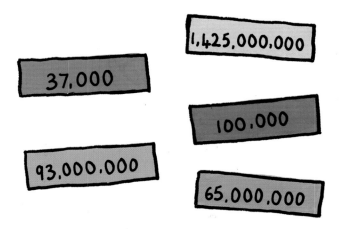

1,425,000,000

37,000

100,000

93,000,000

65,000,000

Do you know many days old you are? You can find the rough answer by multiplying your age by 365 and then adding 2 (if you are 8 or 9). This is because there are 365 days in each year and every four years there is an extra day called a leap year. You might also want to add on the numbers of days that have passed since your last birthday to get an exact answer!

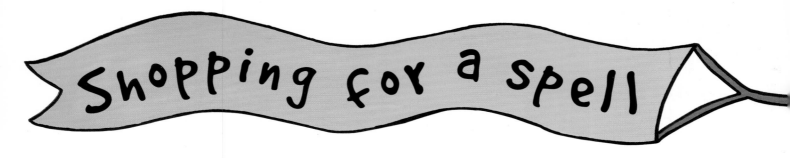

Shopping for a spell

Gruesome Gertie is buying some new ingredients to use in her spells. Here is a page from her catalogue, with the prices of all the things she might need.

Frogs' toes — 10 coins each
Spiders' legs — 2 coins each
Eye of a newt — 6 coins each
Beetles' blood — 3 coins per drop
Dried slugs — 12 coins each
Toenail clippings — 15 coins per bag
Bats' wings — 14 coins per pair

• Which is the most expensive item to buy?

• Which is the cheapest?

• What is the **total** cost in coins?

Here is Gertie's recipe.

• Using the catalogue to guide you, find out how much these ingredients will cost.

Gertie has 100 gold coins to buy the items for her recipe.

• How many coins will she have left if she buys everything she needs?

Make up your own recipe for one of Gruesome Gertie's spells. How many gold coins will it all cost? Will she be able to afford it with only 100 gold coins? Will she have any money left over?

1 Frog's toe
5 Spiders' legs
2 drops of Beetles' blood
1 Dried slug
1 bag of Toenail clippings
1 Bat's wing

The Dublin Chef

Jeff the Chef works in Dublin, in a restaurant.

He has got out enough ingredients to cook for 6 people.

The waiter has just told him that there are **double** the number of people to cook for.

• By doubling, find how much of each ingredient he will now need.

• How much of each ingredient would he need if he was cooking for only 3 people?

How quick are you at doubling numbers up to 30? Write the numbers from 1 to 30 on a piece of paper. Time yourself to see how quickly you can double each number.

Play this game with a friend.

Roll a dice and move forward from the start. If you land on a special square you must double, **halve** or **quarter** the number correctly.

If you make a mistake you must go back three places. See who reaches Jeff the Chef's table first!

Half 16g

Double 28g

Halve 44ml

milk

Quarter of 24ml

Hurry! Jump 2 Squares

Hurry! Jump 2 Squares

Twice 23g

Double 19ml

Flour

Quarter of 16g

Quarter of 48g

Twice 2g

Halve 50m

Half of 14m

Miss a go

Twice 25g

Double 17g

Half of 18g

start

Have another go

Halve 30g

Double 15g

Della, the delivery girl

Della, the delivery girl, is loading her lorry with fruit and vegetables to take to the shops.

Each box contains a different type of fruit or vegetables, such as apples, tomatoes or cabbages.

- How many bags of apples can you see?

- How many boxes of bananas can you see? How many boxes of melons?

- How many apples, bananas and melons are there in each box or bag?

Here is Della's delivery list, showing her how many of each fruit or vegetable she has to deliver today.

She uses the sign x to mean 'lots of' or 'boxes of'. Melons come in boxes of 6, so 2 x 6 melons means 2 'lots of' 6 melons or 2 'boxes of' 6, which is 12 melons altogether.

Delivery Sheet

2 x 6 melons = 12 melons

5 x 10 apples =

5 x 4 cabbages =

2 x 20 cucumbers =

3 x 10 cauliflowers =

3 x 12 bananas =

3 x 8 lettuces =

2 x 12 pineapples =

4 x 8 tomatoes =

Della is working out how many of each item she needs to load on to her lorry.

• Can you help her finish the list?

One-eyed Jake has 24 gold coins. He would like to keep them all, but he knows there are other pirates who will want their share.

Jake thinks of the pirates who might ask for a share and wonders how many coins he will get in each situation.

Look how many coins each pirate will get if there are 2 pirates (Jake and Henry):

Jake gets 12 coins

Henry gets 12 coins

List all the ways you could share out 12 gold coins so that each person has the same amount. (There are five ways of doing this.)

• Now find out how many coins Jake will get if there are:

        3 pirates   4 pirates

• Work out how many coins each pirate will get if there are:

6 pirates   8 pirates   12 pirates

We can write these situations using the **division** sign, like this:

$24 \div 2 = 12$ $24 \div 3 = 8$ $24 \div 4 = 6$ $24 \div 6 = 4$

$24 \div 8 = 3$ $24 \div 12 = 2$

• How many coins would they each get if Jake had 48 coins? Work out:

$48 \div 2 =$ $48 \div 3 =$ $48 \div 4 =$ $48 \div 6 =$

and so on.

Pizza party

Jeff the chef has been cooking pizza. He has cut each pizza into a different number of equal pieces.

Jeff wants to eat one slice of each pizza. A single slice is one 'out of' the total number of slices, for example, '1 out of 4'. We can write this as ¼.

• What **fraction** of each of the following pizzas is one slice?

• How many slices make up half of each pizza?

• What fraction of the mushroom pizza has been eaten and what fraction is left?

Jeff the chef has put some strawberries in bowls for his friends. The numbers show how many strawberries he placed in each bowl.

To find a quarter of a number, find half of a half. Practise finding a quarter of these numbers: 16, 24, 12, 20, 40, 100.

While waiting for his friends, Jeff begins to get hungry.

He starts to eat the strawberries one by one. Soon he has eaten a quarter of the bowl of 8 strawberries.

• How many strawberries has he eaten?

• How many has he left?

• If Jeff eats a quarter of each bowl, how many does he have left in each?

17

The other half

Only half of these pictures is shown. Use a mirror to make these pictures complete.

The image you see in a mirror is called a **reflection**.

On a piece of paper, draw your own half-pictures and use a mirror to complete them.

Lines of symmetry are sometimes called mirror lines.

A symmetrical pattern can be made by folding and cutting paper, like this:

Step 1

Step 2

Step 3

Step 4

Fold a piece of paper in half and cut all four corners off. How many lines of symmetry does your paper have?

• How many times did you fold the paper?

• How many lines of symmetry does this pattern have?

19

Cally the kitchen's Cook

Here are some food items from Cally's kitchen.

- Can you decide which two items are:

The heaviest?   The lightest?   The tallest?   The smallest?

Look closely at the labels.
- How many **grams** does the tin of beans weigh?

- How many **litres** of milk can you see?

- Which object weighs more than one **kilogram**?

- Can you list any other types of measurements?

Find some objects from your kitchen and see how much they weigh, in kilograms or grams. What is the capacity of juice or milk cartons, in litres or millilitres? Make a list of the measurements you find.

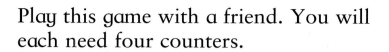

Play this game with a friend. You will each need four counters.

Take it in turns to choose a square.

If you can name any item of the correct size or weight as indicated by the square, put one of your counters on it. The winner is the player who gets four counters in a row.

Taller than 150cm	Heavier than 10kg	3 Litres	10cm	Less than 1cm
Over 1m	Smaller than 20cm	About 1mm	About 150g	Over 1kg
1kg	Lighter than 1kg	Less than 1000ml	Less than 100g	Wider than 30cm
More than 100ml	less than 1 metre	Lighter than 500g	30cm	More than 5kg
About 1cm	500g	Heavier than 2kg	1 Litre	5cm

Coordinate Castle

Welcome to Coordinate Castle. Sir Glancealot, a knight in shining armour, is coming to rescue the princess (not that she needs rescuing!)

To help him, the castle is divided into a grid with **coordinates**. He must visit the coordinates given, to look in lots of rooms to find her.

To find a coordinate he looks at the **grid numbers** along the bottom and up along the side. Sir Glancealot is in grid number (4,1). Can you follow his route? Follow each frame in turn:

(4,1) (4,2) (5,2) (6,2) and across the bridge...

Now go to:
(7,2) (7,1) (8,1) (9,1) (10,1) (11,1)
(12,1) (12,2) (12,3) (11,3) (10,3)
(9,3).

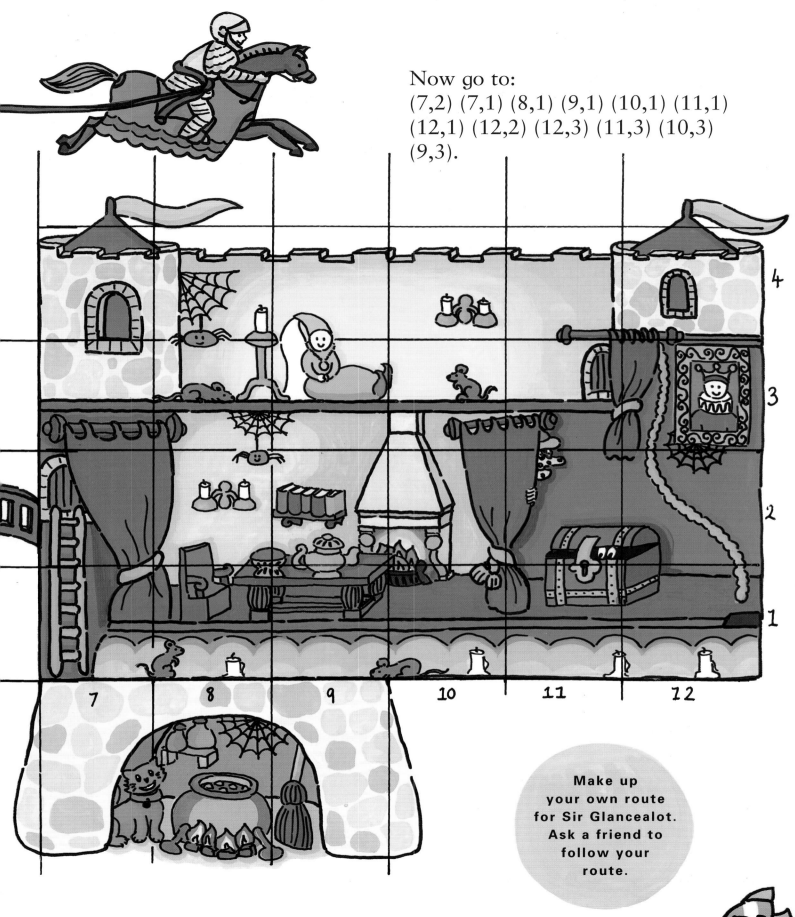

Make up
your own route
for Sir Glancealot.
Ask a friend to
follow your
route.

Fishy business

This cut-out fish is a **right-angle** gobbler. To make a right-angle gobbler:

• Cut out a circle and fold it into 4.

• Open it and cut one quarter out.

• Draw a face and use your gobbler for measuring **angles,** like this:

Angles that are smaller than right angles are called acute angles.

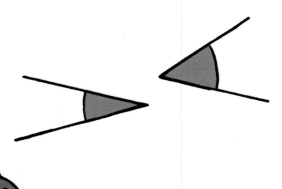

Angles that are larger than right angles and smaller than **straight angles** are called obtuse angles.

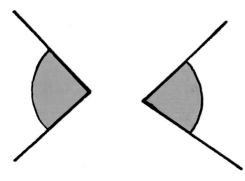

24

These fish have different shaped noses. Some fish have acute-angled noses, some have right-angled noses and some have obtuse-angled noses.

• Can you work out which are which?

Draw some more fish of your own. Write underneath whether the angles are acute, obtuse or right angles.

• How many noses are:
Acute-angled?

Obtuse angled?

Right-angled?

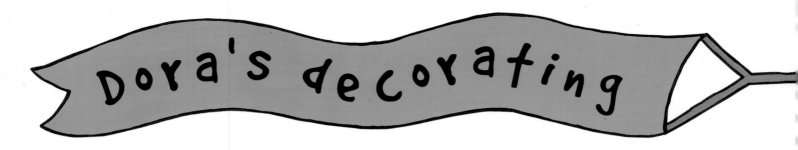

Dora is decorating her house. She has bought some colourful borders to decorate her bedroom. Look at this pattern. Can you see how this pattern has been made?

The basic L shape has been reflected each time in the dotted line.

Here is another pattern that has been made in the same way.

• How would this pattern look if it was continued in the same way?

Trace this pattern and complete it.

These borders have been made by reflecting and **rotating** the shape.

- Can you see how it has been done?

Make up some rotating or reflecting patterns of your own. Make a simple cardboard template and draw around it, turning it or flipping it over as you move along the strip.

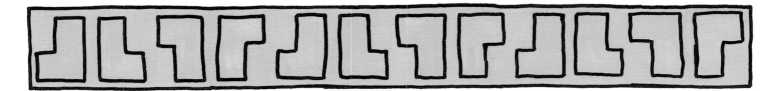

- Try continuing these patterns by drawing them in your notebook.

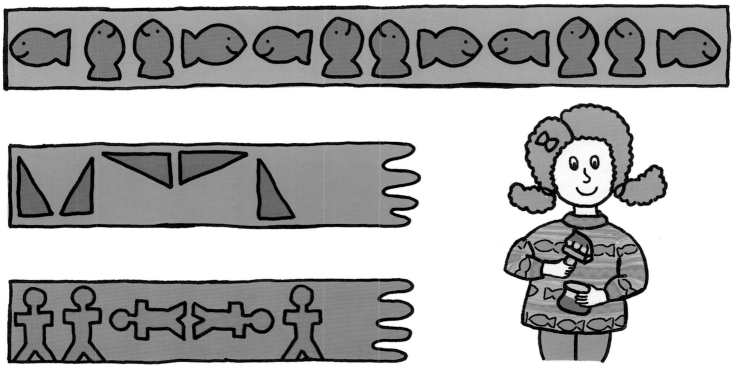

I spy a spy!

Look at these clocks and watches. Some are **digital** and some have clock faces.

- What times do they show?

We use 'am' to show 12 midnight until 12 noon.
This is shown here by a moon symbol.
We use 'pm' from 12 noon to 12 midnight.
This is shown here by a sun symbol.

- Can you see which of the clocks show a time that is 'am' and which show a time that is 'pm'?

Detective Gregory is following a spy. He notes the time and places the spy visits during one day.

- Can you help him by writing down the times?

- What times would it be if the clocks were one hour fast?

Make up your own detective spy story with clocks. Ask a friend to tell you the story!

Glossary

Angle If two lines are joined at one end, the angle is the amount one line has been turned away from the other.

Capacity This is the greatest amount that something can hold.

Coordinates A series of numbers or letters that allow us to pinpoint exactly where something is on a map or graph.

Digital A digital clock uses just numbers rather than putting hands on a clock face.

Division Breaking up something into equal parts.

Double To make twice the number you started with.

Fraction A fraction is a part of something which has been split into equal parts.

Gram A unit of weight; one-thousandth of a kilogram.

Grid numbers The numbers that are used to divide a map or graph into squares.

Halve To break something in two equal parts.

Kilogram A unit of weight made up of one thousand grams.

Line of symmetry If a shape is folded along a line of symmetry one half will cover the other half exactly.

Litre A unit for measuring capacity.

Pattern A design that has been created.

Quarter To divide something in half and then in half again.

Reflection This is an image of something such as the image that can be seen in a mirror.

Right angle This is a quarter of a complete turn. A right angle is sometimes called a square corner.

Rotating This means turning something around from a centre or point.

Straight angle This is an angle that has been opened out flat.

Total This is the answer that we get by adding up a set of numbers. It is also called the 'sum'.

Notes for Adults

Maths is one of the most important subjects to gain a solid understanding of at a young age. This book can be used in school or at home and has been designed to enable children to feel confident in working with numbers, patterns, shapes and angles in a variety of contexts.

The book consists of a series of fun situations, activities and games which build a framework of facts, skills and concepts for Number and Shape work at Lower Key Stage 2. There are also ideas for extension work on each page.

Mathswork 2 meets the main requirements of Lower Key Stage 2 Number and Shape, Space and Measures at Levels 2-4.

Pupils at Key Stage 2 should be able to:
- develop flexible methods and effective methods of computation
- use and apply mathematics in practical tasks, in real-life problems and within mathematics itself
- explore sequences and consider a wide range of patterns
- develop a variety of mental methods of computation and develop their use of the four operations to solve problems, including those involving money and measures
- transform 2D shapes by reflection and rotation and visualise simple transformations to create and describe patterns
- use right angles and fractions of a turn and use the associated language
- choose appropriate standard units of length, mass capacity and time and make sensible estimates with them in everyday situations

This book meets objectives of the National Numeracy Strategy's Framework for Teaching in the following areas:

✓ **Numbers and the number system.**

✓ **Calculations.**

✓ **Handling data.**

✓ **Measures, shape and space.**

Index

Books to read

Mathswork 1 by Steve Mills and Hilary Koll (Wayland, 1999)

At Home with the National Curriculum Learning Workbooks (Letts, 1997)

Holiday (Letts, 1998)

Maths Detectives series (Ladybird, 1998)